Rats For

Amazing Animal Books
For Young Readers
By
Rachel Smith

Mendon Cottage Books

JD-Biz Publishing

All Rights Reserved.

No part of this publication may be reproduced in any form or by any means, including scanning, photocopying, or otherwise without prior written permission from JD-Biz Corp

Copyright © 2014. All Images Licensed by Fotolia and 123RF.

Read More Amazing Animal Books

Purchase at Amazon.com

Table of Contents

Introduction	4
What is a rat?	5
What kinds of rats are there?	7
Where do rats live?	9
The history of rats and humans	11
What is a brown rat?	14
What is a black rat?	17
What is a lab rat?	18
What kinds of lab rats are there?	20
What is a fancy rat and what kinds are there?	22
Conclusion	24
Author Bio	25

Introduction

Rats are some of the most adaptable creatures in the world. It seems like everyone hates them, but they really are interesting and have contributed a lot to science and made good companions for people.

So, are rats all bad? Easy answer, no. But that depends on what type of rat they are, and there are many that should be avoided. Like any animal, some rats are friendly, and others are nasty.

But the rat is an enduring character, inspiring writers from Brian Jacques of the *Redwall* series and E. B. White in *Charlotte's Web* to cast them as nasty, icky villains or at least as unsavory characters. But then again, sometimes rats are portrayed as good characters, such as in Pixar's *Ratatouille*.

In the end, a rat is simply an animal looking for food and shelter.

What is a rat?

A rat is a rodent. It is related to the mouse, but it can be several different sizes, always bigger than the mouse. They are from the genus *Rattus*, which is not Latin for "rat", but is the accepted Latin name for it now.

A rat in grass in a park.

Ancient Romans (who lived a long time ago in Italy) didn't really care much about the differences between mice and rats. They called one 'small mouse' and the other 'big mouse'!

But rats are a different group from mice. They look fairly similar, but in appearance rats have longer snouts, and like it was said before, are bigger.

Rats are also much smarter than mice. They are the smartest kind of rodent, even though there are bigger rodents such as the capybara.

There many kinds of rats throughout the world, and many creatures called rats, but "true rats" include mainly the black rat and the brown rat. Both came from Asia many, many years ago.

A kangaroo rat is not a rat. A pack rat (an American animal) is not a rat. Like with many things, humans simply called them rats because they looked sort of like rats.

There are several names for rats. A female is a doe, and a male is a buck, rather like deer. A pregnant female is a dam. And babies are called pups or kittens. A group of rats is not a herd or a gaggle, but a pack or a mischief of rats.

Rats in general are omnivorous, meaning they will eat almost anything. This is something that has made them the pest of the world.

They also are often nocturnal, coming out to eat at night, when a lot of predators are inactive. In fact, rats are so shy of people, the people often won't know they are inside the house until a chance midnight encounter!

What kinds of rats are there?

There are many, many types of rats.

A mother rat and a young rat.

To start with, there are rats such as the rice field rat, a rat native to Southeast Asia. It tends to be a problem to the farmers there, so they hunt it during the season when the ground is more bare and there are not many places for it to hide. Rice field rat pups have orange tufts behind their ears.

There's also the Polynesian rat, which is the third most widespread rat in the world, behind the brown rat and the black rat. It comes from areas such as Fiji and New Zealand.

There is not a lot of research done on rats outside of the two main ones throughout the world: the brown rat and the black rat.

However, within the brown rat, there are many different kinds of rats descended.

For starters, there are lab rats. Lab rats are specially bred rats that are used for scientific tests. Where at first, there were only albino rats, there are now many different kinds with different kinds of changes made to them through breeding. Some rats are bred for obesity (being very overweight), and some are bred for diabetes, among other things.

And then there is the pet rat. This is called the fancy rat, and it's not like the brown rat it was bred from. A lot of different types of fancy rats are available, from albino to hairless.

Where do rats live?

Rats are almost everywhere!

A black rat.

Perhaps the only continent without rats is Antarctica. Everywhere in the "Old World" (Europe, Asia, and Africa) has its own rats.

Rats were brought over to the "New World" (South and North America, plus sort of Australia) from the Old World on ships hundreds of years ago. The brown rat in particular spread into the Americas.

They have long tormented farm owners by eating the crops, but a lot of rats have become part of urban settings. This means they survive on trash, the food in people's pantries, and other such sources. Most rats don't live in the wilderness nowadays.

The main rats, the black rat and the brown rat, are the most widespread in the world, as mentioned before. If someone in a place like Australia or the United States is talking about wild rats, then they are probably talking about brown rats or black rats.

Rats can live in almost any climate, barring places like the far North Arctic or Antarctica. They are some of the most adaptable creatures in the world, alongside mice and fleas.

They will live anywhere they can get food.

The history of rats and humans

Rats and humans have been at odds for millenia. It is only very recently that anything close to affection for rats has begun. This is partly because rats are not quite the same problem they used to be, at least in first world countries. There is little affection for rats in other parts of the world.

A woman with her pet rat.

As far back as humans began to store food, the fight with the rat (and its cousin, the mouse) has been ongoing.

Especially in third world countries, rats attack crops viciously. In some places, they wipe out entire fields of crops, leaving nothing for poor farmers. Pesticides and other things are used in the first world and second world countries to protect crops; third world farmers generally can't afford these things.

Since rats were such a problem (and still are) in places such as Victorian England and Southeast Asia, the practice of 'ratting' (the hunting of rats) was and is very common. There was and are such populations of rats that even with the great numbers that ratters kill, it seems to make no difference in the damage done by rats.

Rats not only destroy crops, but they destroy buildings and other structures as well. They gnaw into them and can weaken a structure significantly.

Another problem with rats that humans have is the spread of disease. A rat may not directly pass on disease to humans, but their fleas might.

The Black Death (a medieval pandemic) was carried into Europe and elsewhere on the backs of the black rat. Or, rather, in the fleas that had been drinking the black rat's blood. Because conditions weren't very sanitary, the fleas would spread to the people, and they would get very sick.

All of Europe was affected by the Black Death except for Poland. It also affected Asia, spreading throughout the Old World.

This all made the image of the rat a very negative one, even though it was only trying to survive. The rat was cast as the villain in many tales. To be fair to the rat, however, a sewer rat was a nasty creature that no one should have to see or touch, covered in germs and disease. It's also about as friendly as a wild cougar.

A few anecdotes (examples) of rats throughout the world:

In 1780, a Japanese ship wrecked on an island near Alaska. The rats survived, and the place was called Rat Island; it destroyed the local population of birds, because the place was entirely overrun with rats. In 2007, a program started to get rid of all the rats, and in 2009, they seem to have succeeded.

In New Zealand, brown rats were very bad for the local animals. They first arrived about 1800. Nowadays, with an aggressive anti-rat program, the New Zealanders have cleared several islands of rats, and also cleared several areas within the bigger islands of rats.

However, the really interesting story is that of Alberta, Canada. The only kind of rat that could survive in Alberta was the brown rat. Getting there, however, proved to be nearly impossible for a brown rat, due to geography, since Alberta is landlocked and cold, among other things. It wasn't until 1950 that the first brown rat showed up there.

1951, the government had begun a program to get rid of rats. It was probably one of the strongest programs ever enacted; buildings that had rats in them were burned down or exploded, and rats were hunted mercilessly.

Thanks to this program, Alberta is one of the few places in the world without rats.

What is a brown rat?

A brown rat is a basic rat. This is what people think of when they think of rats.

A brown rat.

The brown rat is the most widespread of any rat. It's also where we get every domestic form of rat and every lab rat.

The interesting thing about brown rats is that they have had several names. This is your sewer rat, your street rat, and your common rat. It was also called the Hanover rat at one point in Britain. Hanover is a house (or family) of people that were nobility; calling the brown rat a Hanover rat was supposed to be an insult to the Hanovers.

Another name, the scientific name, is *rattus norvegicus*. It means Norwegian rat, which is very strange because they did not come from Norway. No one is sure why they are called Norwegian rats. It probably really came from China or some part of Central Asia.

A brown rat is a very good swimmer, and pretty nocturnal. They prefer to live anywhere humans are, because they can eat their scraps (or their stores of food). They are not good climbers, however, but they do dig very well. Brown rats will dig very extensive tunnels.

An amazing thing about the brown rat (and other rats) is that they communicate in sounds that humans can't hear. This is known as an ultrasonic vocalization, or a sound outside of the range of human hearing. Human hearing is really not all that good compared to a rat's.

A baby rat will make ultrasonic sounds, but eventually stops doing it around male rats because they don't want to be hurt by them. Rats also use ultrasonic sounds to communicate danger to each other.

Rats like these will also chirp, another sound that humans can't hear. This seems to mean they're laughing, or else expecting something good, such as tickling or feeding time.

However, brown rats also make sounds that humans can hear. One, which sounds a lot like teeth grinding, is called burring. Rats make it when they're happy, or when they are trying to soothe themselves sometimes.

Rats also squeak, but only because of pain or fear. A rat squeaking could be in great pain, or it could feel threatened. It is never a sign that they are happy or trying to communicate with each other.

According to studies done in the 1960's, brown rats enjoy scrambled eggs, macaroni and cheese, and cooked corn. However, brown rats will eat anything that is edible, from meat to grain to the strangest of human concoctions. They especially like chocolate.

Brown rats will live in both packs and family groups. They will sleep together, huddle together (which seems to be a way to stay warm) and play together. There is an order of dominance (who's in charge) throughout the pack, and sometimes rats will fight about dominance.

When brown rats play fight, they will seem to go for each other's necks; however, they aren't trying to harm the rat. It's only for fun. When they go for the other rat's rear, however, that's when things are serious.

Mother brown rats can have up to five litters a year. Baby brown rats need their mother's warmth, since they can't keep themselves warm.

The brown rat carries many germs, including some that spread to predators such as cats and get carried to humans. The brown rat has a system that is somewhat similar to a human's, and so diseases that affect it often affect humans too.

What is a black rat?

The black rat is also one of the most common rats in the world, and sort of the source of the Black Death back in medieval times. As mentioned before, they carried the disease in the fleas that were on their bodies.

It is called *rattus rattus*, and it also came from Asia, more specifically Southeast Asia. However, this was a much longer time ago than the brown rat; black rats have been in Europe since prehistoric times (meaning times before we have a written history).

The black rat has been called by many names, including roof rat, ship rat, and Alexandrine rat. It is a bit smaller than the brown rat, and was pushed a bit out of its space by the brown rat. It is also known as the Old English rat, because before the brown rats showed up, the black rats were all that were in England.

Black rats are generalist omnivores, which means they will eat just about anything. They like fruits and nuts best, but have been known to eat feed for animals such as cows and dogs.

The black rat is not as widespread as the brown rat for several reasons. The first is that the brown rat can survive in cooler climates than the black rat can. The second is that, as buildings changed from dirt and straw to concrete and stone, brown rats could more easily make homes in urban places by burrowing than the black rat could by living making dens in trees or on the ground.

Black rats can climb much better than brown rats, and this gives them an advantage in more wild settings. The black rat never settled much in North America, unlike the brown rat. However, they are present in places such as India and Southeast Asia in great numbers.

What makes the black rat a real pest is that at times, the population (number of rats) will explode, and they will completely consume farmers' crops, leaving them with nothing to eat.

It causes many of the same problems as the brown rat does.

What is a lab rat?

The lab rat is a descendant of the brown rat. It is an animal used to test scientific theories on.

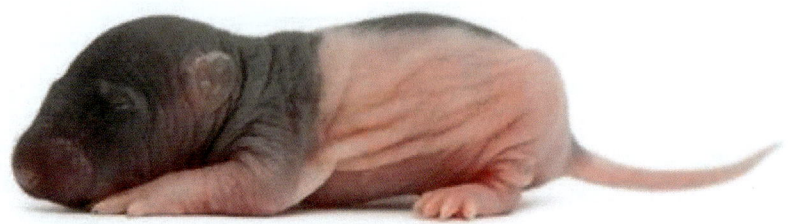

A baby rat.

The thing that makes a rat so perfect for tests is that it has a rather similar system compared to a human, and it can catch many of the same diseases.

The origin of the lab rat is a bit muddled. Back in the 1800s, there was an enormous population of rats in the streets and homes of Britain. So, the practice of ratting again came into popularity; these rats were captured, and then used for food or for rat-baiting.

Rat-baiting was a cruel game where a terrier dog was unleashed on a bunch of captured rats, and men bet on how long it would take the dog to kill them all.

However, eventually some rat-catchers began to breed rats for these games, and they ended up with new varieties, such as hooded (with brown or black over their head and neck, and the rest white) and albino. The theory is that these rats were used to test theories, the first being one on fasting.

Another theory is that these lab rats came from Japan. In the 1700s and into the 1800s, a trend in Japan was to have a pet rat. They were bred for special characteristics, such as albinism (complete lack of pigment, or color), and it's said that all albino lab rats are descended from a single rat from Japan, brought over by Japanese people.

In any case, the lab rat is an important part of the laboratory setting.

What kinds of lab rats are there?

There are many kinds of lab rats developed from the few that started in out back in the early 1800s.

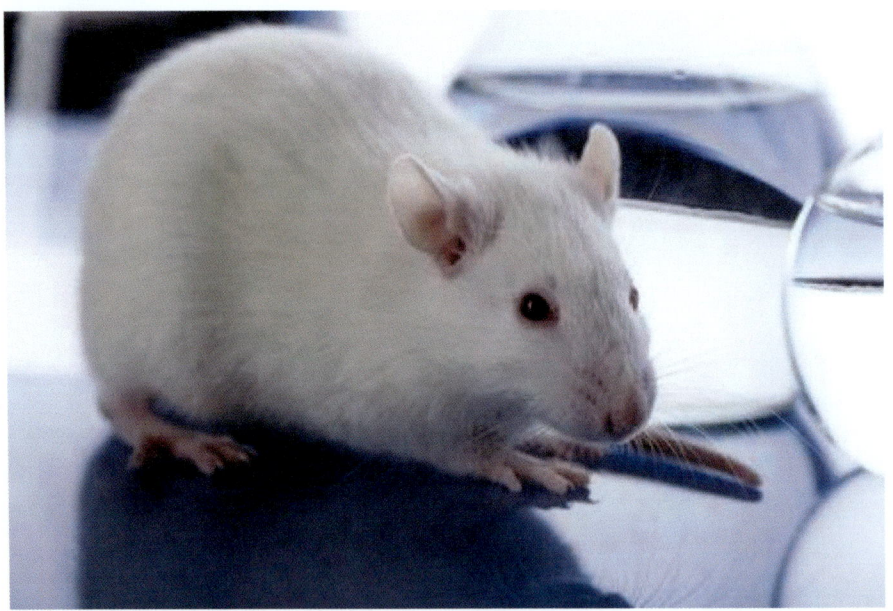

A lab rat.

The Wistar rat is the basic albino. It is the first breed designed to be a model organism. It was bred back in the early 1900s. Many other kinds were developed from this breed.

A Sprague-Dawley rat is bred from the Wistar rat. It's used in medical research because it is particularly calm and easy to handle.

The Biobreeding rat is made to develop type 1 diabetes, and it helps doctors figure out how to handle diabetes cases. Meanwhile, the Zucker rat is designed to get very fat, and is used as a model to study obesity (extremely overweight) and hypertension.

Hairless rats are best for testing out ideas about immune systems.

These are just a few of the types developed by scientists, but the important thing to know is that they are not allowed to seriously suffer. In the old days, perhaps just fifty years ago, scientists could do what they wanted to lab rats with impunity (no punishment).

Now, lab rats are treated more kindly, and they aren't used to test cruel hypotheses (ideas).

What is a fancy rat and what kinds are there?

A fancy rat is a pet rat. Like the lab rat, it developed from the brown rat.

A fancy rat outdoors.

Like the lab rat also, it started out in the bloody games that were played in the 1800s; when people started breeding different kinds of rats, however, interest in them as pets soared.

A man named Jack Black, who was Queen Victoria's rat catcher, began to breed rats to make prettier colors and the like. It became quite the craze among the upper class to have a fancy rat; women would cover them in ribbons and then have them on little leashes on their laps.

The 'rat fancy' (meaning a want for a pet rat) lasted until about the 1920's to 1930's, and it fell out of fashion then. It took a while for rats to become somewhat more mainstream pets again, until 1976, when a new rat breeding group was founded.

The important thing to know about fancy rats is that there are none of the same dangers as with wild rats; they have been bred to be less likely to bite, and they are not prone to the same diseases. A bite from a fancy rat is unlikely to lead to anything serious, should it ever be scared enough to bite.

Fancy rats have been found to be able to teach tricks; some can learn to respond to their name, and others can be litter box trained.

There are a lot of names for different fur patterns, from hooded to capped or Berkshire. There are also different fur types, from curly to satiny to normal.

Two kinds of rats with different bodies include the Dumbo, a rat with much larger ears, and the Manx, a rat with no tail.

Lastly, there are hairless rats, which can have a very fine, thin coat of hair, or none at all. They are mutants, like the Manx and the Dumbo.

Conclusion

Rats are probably more interesting creatures than most people realize. While they have contributed to things such as famine and plague, the rat itself is not to blame. Like any animal, it just wants to live.

And live it has; it covers almost every corner of the earth.

Rats make excellent pets, study subjects, and favorite animals. They are clever enough to act in movies, and smart enough to learn to love their owners with great affection.

Rats are, and will never cease to be, a constant in our world.

Author Bio

Rachel Smith is a young author who enjoys animals. Once, she had a rabbit who was very nervous, and chewed through her leash and tried to escape. She's also had several pet mice, who were the funniest little animals to watch. She lives in Ohio with her family and writes in her spare time.

Our books are available at

1. Amazon.com

2. Barnes and Noble

3. Itunes

4. Kobo

5. Smashwords

6. Google Play Books

This book is published by

JD-Biz Corp

P O Box 374

Mendon, Utah 84325

http://www.jd-biz.com/

Top Ten
Dog Breeds
For Kids
Amazing Animal Books
For Young Readers
Kisha Bennett & John Davidson

Poodles
Dog Books for Kids
K. Bennett

Labrador
Retrievers
Dog Books for Kids
K. Bennett

German Shepherds
Dog Books for Kids
K. Bennett

Rottweilers
Dog Books for Kids
K. Bennett

Boxers
Dog Books for Kids
K. Bennett

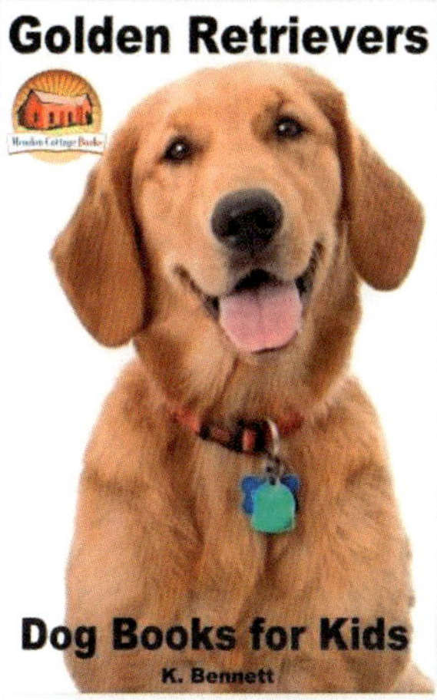
Golden Retrievers
Dog Books for Kids
K. Bennett

Beagles
Dog Books for Kids
K. Bennett

Yorkies
Dog Books for Kids
K. Bennett

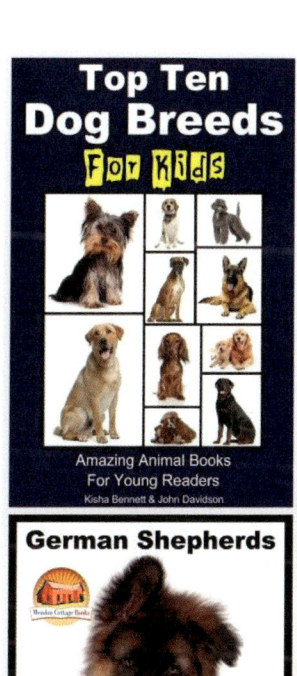

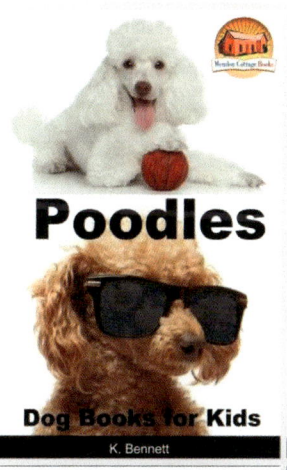

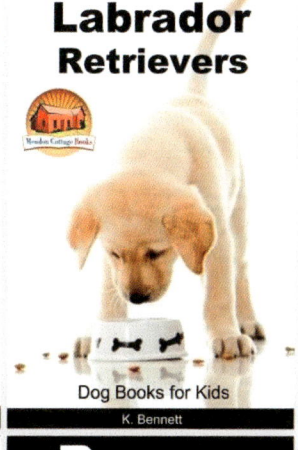

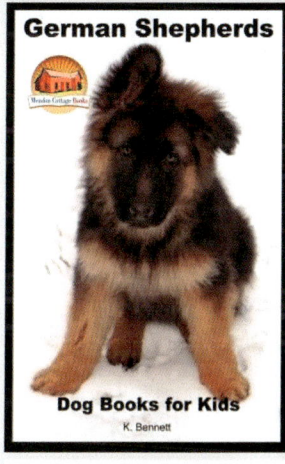

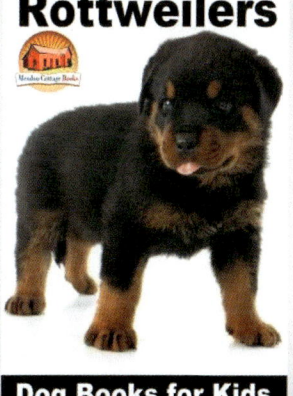

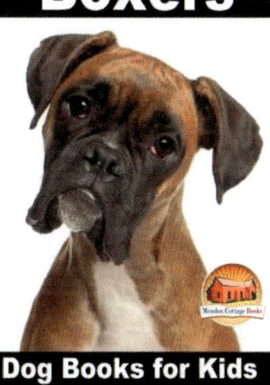

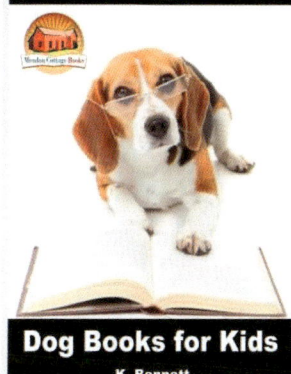

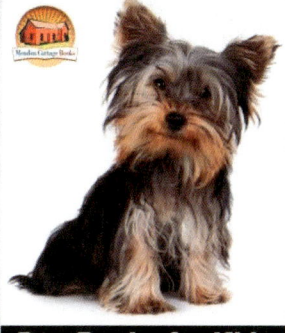

Rats Page 29

Printed in Great
Britain
by Amazon